Piano Concerto No. 5
in E-flat Major, Op. 73
"Emperor"

Ludwig van Beethoven

DOVER PUBLICATIONS, INC.
Mineola, New York

Contents

Dedicated to His Imperial Majesty, Archduke Rudolph

The concerto was premiered on 28 November 1811, in Leipzig. Its first performance in Vienna took place on 12 February 1812, at the opera house, in honor of the Emperor's birthday, with Carl Czerny as soloist. For the unveiling of the Beethoven monument in Bonn, in 1845, Franz Liszt—who was instrumental in raising money for that edifice—appeared as soloist in a public performance of the work. The label "Emperor" was unknown in Beethoven's lifetime.

Piano Concerto No. 5
in E-flat Major, Op. 73,
"Emperor"

(1809)

INSTRUMENTATION

2 Flutes [Flauti, Fl.]

2 Oboes [Oboi, Ob.]

2 Clarinets in A, B♭("B") [Clarinetti, Clar.]

2 Bassoons [Fagotti, Fag.]

2 Horns in D, E♭("Es") [Corni, Cor.]

2 Trumpets in E♭("Es") [Trombe, Tr.]

Timpani [Timpani, Timp.]

Piano Solo [Pianoforte]

Violins I, II [Violino]

Violas [Viola]

Cellos [Violoncello, Vlc.]

Basses [Basso, Cb.]

Piano Concerto No. 5

in E-flat Major, Op. 73
"Emperor"

I

352

357

480

486

NB. Non si fa una Cadenza, ma s'attacca subito il seguente.

II

NB. Semplice poco tenuto.

III